CLEOPATRA
The Last Great Queen of Egypt

CLEOPATRA
The Last Great Queen of Egypt

An Epic Adventure for Kids
About the Pharaoh Who Defied Rome

Samuel C. A.

Cleopatra: The Last Great Queen of Egypt
First edition: April, 2025

© 2025, Samuel C. A.
The author has reserved all rights.
Please contact the copyright holders.

Printed on demand

Note: All rights reserved. No part of this work may be reproduced, incorporated into a computer system, or transmitted in any form or by any means (electronic, mechanical, photocopying, recording, or otherwise) without the prior written permission of the copyright holders. Infringement of such rights may constitute an intellectual property crime.

contacto@samueljohnbooks.com

WHAT'S INSIDE?

Prologue: The Legacy of a Queen. 9

The Young Princess of Egypt 13

The Exile of a Queen: The Trial of the Desert 19

The Return to Egypt and the Battle for the Throne 23

The Rise and Triumph of a Queen 29

The Shadow of Rome and Mark Antony 35

The Battle of Actium. 41

The Last Battle of Cleopatra. 47

Epilogue: A Legacy Never Forgotten. 53

Fun Facts About Cleopatra 59

Cleopatra's Timeline 61

Questions to Reflect and Discuss 63

Cleopatra's Mini Glossary 65

References. 69

PROLOGUE
THE LEGACY OF
A QUEEN

The dawn bathed the city of Alexandria in a golden glow. The air was thick with excitement. A gentle breeze carried the salty scent of the Mediterranean, mingling with the perfume of spices from the marketplace. For most of its people, it was just another day. But not for a small group of children gathered eagerly in the shade of ancient columns. Their eyes, filled with curiosity, shone with the thrill of the unknown.

Among them stood an old storyteller. The wrinkles on his face were the marks of a life devoted to telling tales. His deep and captivating voice held the power to carry listeners across the sands of time. That morning, they were about to embark on an unforgettable adventure unlike any other.

"Come closer, little ones," said the old man, his gaze full of mystery. "Today, I shall tell you about Cleopatra. She was not just a queen. She was a warrior, a scholar, and a strategist. She wove her life with threads of courage and wisdom."

The children inched closer, captivated by the mystery of his words. In their minds, they could already hear the clash of swords and feel the weight of a golden crown.

"Cleopatra's story begins long before she became a queen," the old man continued, leaning forward as if about to share a secret. "She was born in a land bathed by the sun and the golden sands of Egypt, a kingdom of wisdom and legends. From a young age, she had an insatiable desire to learn and discover the unknown."

The children imagined her wandering through the grand Library of Alexandria, her eyes fixed on ancient scrolls, her fingers gliding across texts filled with stories of distant lands.

"But what made Cleopatra truly extraordinary," the old man said, "was her spirit. Ever since childhood, she dreamed of a world she could change. She feared no challenge that stood in her way."

The children pictured her as a heroine: bold, determined, ready to carve her path in history.

PROLOGUE: THE LEGACY OF A QUEEN

"She learned the art of ruling, not only from books but through experience," said the old man, raising a hand to give more drama to the tale. "Imagine a world of warring kingdoms where this young woman was willing to lead with intelligence and bravery."

His words carried them to halls filled with advisors and battlefields where banners fluttered in the wind. And there stood Cleopatra: listening, learning, preparing for the day when destiny would call her to reign.

"But even amid greatness, Cleopatra never ceased to be herself," the old man added, his voice softening. "She learned languages, helped her people, and never forgot her roots. Her heart was as vast as the Nile River."

The children smiled as they imagined her so wise and strong. They saw in her not just a queen but a person with dreams and worries, not so different from themselves.

"So, my young friends," said the storyteller with a warm smile, "this is how Cleopatra's story begins. A journey full of triumphs and true challenges, a proof that within each of you, there is a strength capable of changing the world."

Silence wrapped around them. The children sat spellbound, feeling the old storyteller's words reach deep into their hearts.

"Now, listen carefully," said the old man with a soft chuckle as he settled among them. "Get ready, for I am about to tell you the true story of a queen who defied fate and carved her name into eternity."

The children huddled closer, excitement and anticipation shining in their eyes. Cleopatra's story was about to begin, and no one wanted to miss a single word.

THE YOUNG PRINCESS OF EGYPT

Though she lived surrounded by luxury, Cleopatra's most significant treasure was not jewels or royal banquets—it was knowledge. From a very young age, Cleopatra felt an immense passion for learning everything about her world and firmly believed she was destined for greatness.

Her home was no ordinary palace; it was the royal palace of Alexandria, a majestic place where decisions were made that shaped the fate of entire nations. Cleopatra grew up watching and learning among golden columns and perfumed gardens. She was unlike other noble children who were content with the pleasures of palace life. No—she longed to understand the world's secrets, unlock the mysteries hidden in ancient books, and learn from the wisest people of her time.

Cleopatra Awakens

From the time she was a child, Cleopatra stood out within the grand royal palace. Unlike her siblings, she possessed a rare blend of intelligence and curiosity that set her apart. Her eyes sparkled whenever she discovered something new, and she always craved to learn more—even things others thought too difficult for someone her age. While other princes and princesses enjoyed the comforts of palace life, Cleopatra preferred to explore the world around her, always searching for answers.

One of Cleopatra's most astonishing talents was her gift for languages. While other children struggled to speak their tongue fluently, Cleopatra had already mastered Egyptian, Greek, and several languages from distant lands. Thanks to this, she could converse with scholars, merchants, and rulers worldwide. To Cleopatra, every language was a doorway to a world of knowledge, where she could uncover the secrets of philosophy, science, and history. Her mind was like a sponge, absorbing everything she heard and read, an extraordinary feat even for a princess.

For Cleopatra, learning was not just a pastime but

the path to her true destiny. Ever since she was little, she dreamed of ruling Egypt with wisdom and justice. She did not seek power simply because of her birthright; she knew knowledge would be the key to becoming a great leader. She did not hide her desire to reign or wait for fate to decide for her. Cleopatra did not want to be just another heir—she wanted to be a Pharaoh who would lead her people to greatness.

Among the palace's luxuries and mysteries, Cleopatra's dream of ruling grew stronger every day. Lavish banquets welcomed ambassadors from distant lands, golden halls shone with the glow of torchlight, and music filled the corridors. Yet behind those feasts and smiles, there were secrets and betrayals.

In that world, Cleopatra learned that being a ruler was not just about wearing a crown. To lead meant to be clever, to think strategically, and always to stay one step ahead of her enemies. She watched her father, Pharaoh Ptolemy XII, fight to keep his throne amidst constant threats. She learned a crucial lesson from him: power was never guaranteed—it had to be protected, and a single mistake could cost her the kingdom. It was not enough to dream of the throne; she would have to prove herself worthy of it. More than just a queen, Cleopatra wished to become a leader prepared to face any challenge.

Cleopatra took full advantage of her privileged position to learn and strengthen her knowledge. Her talent for languages and curiosity for other cultures widened her view of the world. From an early age, she knew that being different was not a weakness but her greatest strength, and she was determined to use her intelligence to become a great leader.

The Birth of a Leader

Although Cleopatra was sure she wanted to be a great ruler who would lead Egypt into a prosperous future, there was one problem: at that time, it was rare for a woman to rule alone. Most queens had to marry a man who would rule beside them. But Cleopatra had other plans. She would not allow anyone else to make decisions for her. Cleopatra was determined to prove that a queen could be decisive, wise, and just without depending on anyone. Her destiny was not to follow someone else's rules but to carve her own path.

Inspired by the ancient kings of Egypt, she set out to learn everything necessary to become the best ruler possible. She studied military strategy, learned how to negotiate with diplomats, understood the importance of trade, and discovered why the Nile was the key to her people's wealth. She knew that fate would put her to the test one day, and she needed to be ready.

The palace was full of mysteries, and the threats never ceased. Her father continued to fight to keep his throne, but Cleopatra clearly saw that her time would come sooner or later. She knew the day she would have to fight for Egypt drew closer.

While her siblings enjoyed wealth and power without a care in the world, Cleopatra had a plan. She would not sit idly by, waiting for destiny to decide. She would forge her own path, using her intelligence, courage, and unbreakable will.

And so, the young princess, who had once been just a curious child, was preparing to become the last great Pharaoh of Egypt.

An Extraordinary Destiny

Although Cleopatra would one day grow to become one of the most legendary figures in history, in those early years—before the great battles, before the alliances with emperors, before her name was written in the history books—she was simply a girl with a powerful dream: to rule with wisdom and justice.

She did not want to be remembered only for her beauty or being born into a powerful family but for her intelligence and ability to be a great leader.

And so her story began—the story of a young princess who would defy destiny and change the course of history forever.

THE EXILE OF A QUEEN
THE TRIAL OF THE DESERT

In ancient Egypt, the royal family's life was as unpredictable as a sandstorm. From a young age, Cleopatra grew up amidst an endless struggle for the throne. And finally, the dreaded day arrived. The enemies of Ptolemy XII achieved their goal: the Pharaoh was overthrown and driven out of Alexandria, betrayed by those who had once sworn loyalty to him. With his fall, chaos erupted within the royal family, trapping Cleopatra and her siblings in an uncertain fate, forced to face a future without the king's protection. Like the ever-shifting dunes of the desert, Cleopatra's life changed without rest.

The palace, once a safe refuge, became a dangerous

place. Cleopatra and her sister Arsinoe realized there was only one choice: to flee. Leaving behind the luxury of Alexandria, they embarked on a perilous journey across the vast and unforgiving desert, heading toward Syria.

Their escape marked the beginning of a voyage that would test their strength and wits. Cleopatra was not only leaving behind the splendor of the palace, but she would also discover within herself a strength she never imagined she possessed.

The journey became a harsh trial of endurance. During the day, the scorching sun punished them; at night, the freezing wind wrapped around them like a deadly threat. Water was scarce, food barely enough, and bandits lurked in the shadows of the dunes, ready to attack. What should have been a journey of days stretched into endless weeks of suffering, where every step was a battle against exhaustion and fear.

But the desert did not only test their physical endurance—it also shaped their spirit. Without the palace's comforts, Cleopatra had to adapt quickly. Among the endless dunes, she learned to read the land, deal with travelers, and survive in a world where every step could be her last.

Despite the hardships, Cleopatra never gave up. Her desire to reclaim her place in the world drove her forward. The young princess did not simply survive the desert; she emerged stronger and more determined than ever. What began as a desperate escape turned into the first great trial of her destiny — the forging of the leader Egypt was waiting for.

Survival and Leadership in the Desert

Cleopatra's true journey began when, in the heart of the desert, she encountered the Bedouin nomads. Far from the luxury of Alexandria, these travelers knew how to survive in one of the world's harshest environments. To Cleopatra, they were not just companions on the road — they were teachers who shared the most valuable lessons: how to adapt, endure, and lead.

The Bedouins did not rule from ivory thrones. Their power lay in shared wisdom, cooperation, and the determination to face the unknown. Cleopatra watched, learned, and understood that authentic leadership is not imposed through fear but earned through respect and cunning.

Cleopatra spent sleepless nights under the starry desert sky, lost in thought. As the fire crackled and the wind whispered among the dunes, she grasped the weight of betrayal and the long road still ahead. From the top of a hill, she gazed upon the vast land she would one day rule. And there, with a steady voice, she made a promise — a promise that only the desert heard:

"I will return... and I will rule."

But it would not be for revenge alone but for the burning desire in her heart to restore greatness to her people. At that moment, Cleopatra ceased to be a mere fugitive and became a future queen, ready to claim her destiny.

Every obstacle on her path strengthened her, bringing her closer to the fate that awaited her. Surviving the desert became her first great trial as a leader. Every sandstorm made her stronger, every sleepless night taught her to wait for the right moment, and every hardship forced her to think before acting. The journey's hardships erased every trace of weakness, leaving behind an unbreakable will. When she finally set foot in Syria, Cleopatra was no longer the young princess who had escaped Egypt — she was a woman forged by struggle, with one purpose in mind: to reclaim her throne and leave her mark on history.

THE RETURN TO EGYPT AND THE BATTLE FOR THE THRONE

The throne of Egypt was as unstable as a ship caught in the middle of a storm. After Ptolemy XII was overthrown, Egypt sank into chaos. Yet, the old pharaoh was not ready to vanish without a fight. With the help of the Romans, he reclaimed his throne. But his victory came at a high price. He became deeply indebted to Rome, and the Romans took advantage of this to tighten their grip on Egypt. Ptolemy XII was pharaoh once again, but he no longer ruled freely. Now, he ruled under the looming shadow of Rome.

Time was running against him. Ptolemy XII was sick and weak and died shortly after regaining the throne. His death unleashed a new struggle for power.

Following tradition, Cleopatra, his eldest daughter, inherited the crown but had to share it with her younger brother, Ptolemy XIII. Yet, in Egypt, sharing power had never been easy. The siblings did not trust each other, and it quickly became apparent that neither would give up the throne without a fight.

The inexperience and immaturity of Ptolemy XIII clashed with Cleopatra's intelligence and determination, making it impossible for them to rule peacefully. The palace advisors took advantage of this, quickly manipulating the young pharaoh and pushing Cleopatra away from the throne. In the end, they succeeded in driving her out of Egypt. But Cleopatra refused to give up. She began preparing for her return from exile, armed with courage and cleverness.

Cleopatra's Fight for Power

Cleopatra did not see her exile as a defeat but as an opportunity. Without wasting time on sadness or regret, the young queen turned her exile into part of a grand plan to return stronger than ever. Slowly but surely, Cleopatra gathered a loyal group of followers who believed in her and shared her dream for Egypt. Her bravery and leadership inspired these men and women to stand by her side, ready to do whatever it took to help her reclaim the throne.

While away from Egypt, Cleopatra watched as Rome, growing ever more powerful, spread its influence across the Mediterranean. She knew that if she wished to return to power, she would need the support of the Romans. She could not afford to return to Egypt without powerful allies, and she found the key to her return to Rome.

What seemed like a disaster soon became a great opportunity. During her exile, Cleopatra gathered allies, sharpened her plans, and prepared herself to return stronger than ever. What began as an escape was another step leading her closer to her true destiny: to become the bravest and wisest queen Egypt had ever known.

The Arrival of Julius Caesar

The ancient world was full of secrets, dangers, and ever-changing alliances. Power was gained through cleverness, courage, and, many times, through bloody battles. Cleopatra fought to reclaim her rightful place in the middle of it all. But her path was filled with enemies and obstacles. Then, fate placed before her a man who would change her life forever: Julius Caesar, one of Rome's most powerful generals, had come with the mission to bring order and secure Egypt's loyalty to Rome.

While Cleopatra was still in Syria, news reached her that Julius Caesar, the great Roman general, had arrived in Alexandria. Though returning meant risking her life, Cleopatra knew this was her chance to take back the throne. Determined to act quickly and wisely, she secretly crossed the desert until she reached Egypt.

Caesar had come to enforce Rome's demands. His arrival was a friendly visit and a clear warning: Egypt must show loyalty and obedience to Rome or face the consequences.

For Cleopatra, Caesar's arrival was both a great danger and a priceless opportunity. She knew that her brother, Ptolemy XIII, had the full support of the influential palace advisors, who would do anything to keep her away from the throne. If Cleopatra wished to reclaim Egypt, she needed a strong ally. However, approaching the Roman general would not be easy. Caesar was surrounded by soldiers and politicians who trusted no one. Still, Cleopatra was determined. She would do whatever it took to reach him and prove that she was the true queen of Egypt.

Storytellers have shared how Cleopatra met Caesar for centuries: she was secretly brought to him, hidden inside a rolled-up carpet. This daring entrance showed not only her bravery but also her cleverness. Cleopatra wanted to prove to the mighty Roman general that she was bold and sharp, ready to do whatever it took to fulfill her goal. Caesar was amazed by the young Egyptian queen's wit and courage.

A simple meeting between two leaders quickly

THE RETURN TO EGYPT AND THE BATTLE FOR THE THRONE

turned into a powerful alliance. With Caesar's support, Cleopatra gathered the strength to face her enemies and reclaim her throne. However, this alliance also came with significant risks. In Rome, many distrusted Cleopatra and saw her as a threat to the balance of Roman power. Yet Cleopatra was ready to face any danger to fulfill her destiny.

While Rome was tearing itself apart in a civil war between its generals, Cleopatra moved carefully and wisely, using her relationship with Julius Caesar to secure her place on the throne. She knew well that ruling was not just about placing a crown on her head — it meant defending it with courage so that no one could ever take it away again.

THE RISE AND TRIUMPH OF A QUEEN

That day dawned differently over Alexandria. The sun seemed to know that something important was about to happen, shining on the waters of the Nile with a special glow. The usually calm banks seemed to tremble with excitement, and in the air, you could almost feel that something extraordinary was about to unfold.

From a nearby hill, Cleopatra watched it all. In the distance, her ships prepared to face her brother, the young Pharaoh Ptolemy XIII. The Egyptian troops, joined by Julius Caesar's powerful Roman forces, stood firm, waiting for the signal. With calm and determination, Cleopatra slowly raised her arm, showing that the moment had come to fight for Egypt.

In a matter of seconds, the calm vanished. The battle began, and dozens of ships rushed forward along the Nile. The sound of drums echoed everywhere, setting the rhythm of the combat, while arrows traced thin golden lines in the sky, shining like shooting stars under the blazing sun.

The battle was fierce and terrible. Egyptian and Roman ships crashed hard against Ptolemy's fleet, which soon began to break apart and catch fire. The river quickly filled with broken pieces of wood floating on the water while flames rose high into the sky, forming thick columns of dark smoke visible from every corner of Alexandria. From afar, Cleopatra watched calmly, fully convinced that this was the only way to restore peace to Egypt.

Meanwhile, on the other side of the battle, Ptolemy XIII watched in fear as his soldiers began to lose. His youth and inexperience were no match for Cleopatra's intelligence and cleverness, strengthened by the might of the Roman army. Unable to control his panic, the young pharaoh rushed to a small boat, desperate to escape and save his life.

But the tiny boat could not hold the weight of so many terrified men. It suddenly flipped, throwing Ptolemy into the water. There, in the depths of the Nile — the river that had always given life to Egypt — the young pharaoh met his fate, ending a struggle that had torn the kingdom apart for far too long.

The Triumphal Return to Alexandria

The battle had been short but decisive. With the enemy defeated, Alexandria, weary of war, opened its gates wide for the young Cleopatra, who entered the city on a magnificent golden chariot. As she passed, the streets filled with citizens who showered her path with flowers, finally recognizing the brave young woman as their true pharaoh. Cleopatra, her head held high, proud and calm, smiled at her people, knowing that this moment marked the beginning of her reign.

The city gathered in Alexandria's great temple that afternoon to witness the coronation ceremony. Inside, the scent of incense floated through the air, mixing with the sweet aroma of freshly cut flowers. Priests dressed in white robes moved slowly forward, carrying Egypt's sacred symbols. Cleopatra walked along a path covered with petals until she reached the main altar, where she received the double crown — the symbol of the union between Upper and Lower Egypt.

When the crown gently touched her head, Cleopatra felt the great responsibility of all Egypt resting on her shoulders. Yet, instead of fear, a deep sense of confidence filled her heart. She knew she was ready to lead her people toward a brighter future. Around her, everyone bowed respectfully, accepting her as the last great pharaoh of Egypt.

Destiny Fulfilled

Nightfall came quickly, covering Alexandria beneath a sky full of stars. After a long and exhausting day, Cleopatra slowly climbed up to a balcony of the royal palace. From there, she gazed at the city that was now hers. She looked at the streets lit by hundreds of small lamps, at the houses where families slept peacefully, and at the Nile River, calm once again, shining under the moon's light.

Cleopatra remembered all that she had lived through in the stillness of the night: her childhood in the palace, her exile in the desert, the trials that had made her stronger, and, at last, the brave battle to win back her rightful place. Every obstacle had been another stone that the queen Egypt needed.

She also considered the future, fully aware that new challenges would surely come. She knew she would have to be even cleverer and stronger than ever, for her throne would not be free of dangers or threats. But Cleopatra felt no fear, for she trusted deeply in herself and the people she now led.

At that moment, as she gazed at the stars shining above the sleeping city, a deep sense of fulfillment filled her heart. She had kept her promise long ago in the desert when, far from home, she dreamed of regaining what was hers. She had returned and fought, and now, at last, she had triumphed.

With a proud smile, Cleopatra took a deep breath, letting the cool night air fill her lungs. Below her, the city slept peacefully, perhaps unaware that its destiny had changed forever that very day.

In the silence of the night, Cleopatra softly whispered, firm and determined, words that summed up all she had achieved and all that this moment meant to her:

"Egypt is mine."

And so, under the moon's silver glow, a new chapter began in the life of the young queen who had chosen to take control of her destiny, leading her people toward a future worthy of being remembered forever.

THE SHADOW OF ROME
AND MARK ANTONY

After her triumphant return to Egypt, Cleopatra ruled with determination, but deep down, she sensed that her power remained fragile and uncertain. Julius Caesar had helped her reclaim the throne; together, they even had a son, Caesarion, a living proof of their bond. Yet Cleopatra could never fully trust Rome. It was a treacherous place, capable of breaking promises in the blink of an eye and getting rid of a ruler with a single dagger strike.

One day, news struck Alexandria like lightning: Roman senators had assassinated Julius Caesar in the Senate of Rome. Cleopatra was stunned. Her greatest ally, the man who had helped her regain her throne, was gone. A storm of questions filled her mind: What would happen to Egypt now? Was her kingdom in danger? What would Rome do next? She knew that nothing would ever be the same and that she had to be ready for whatever was coming.

Rome was in chaos. Its leaders were fighting among themselves, each one trying to seize power. From Egypt, Cleopatra watched closely, waiting for the perfect moment to act. Soon, a new leader rose to fame in Rome: Mark Antony, a brave and clever warrior who had been Julius Caesar's most loyal friend. The moment Cleopatra learned of him, she knew he could be the key to protecting her kingdom. If she could earn his trust, together they could make Egypt stronger and face whatever new dangers appeared.

And so, Cleopatra prepared herself for the meeting with the man who would once again change her destiny.

The Meeting of Cleopatra and Mark Antony

Cleopatra's arrival was a spectacle worthy of the gods. Her majestic ship sailed slowly down the river, its purple sails billowing in the wind and its golden stern shining brightly, like the sun itself, leaving everyone who saw it wide-eyed with wonder. Standing on the deck, dressed in a dazzling robe, she looked like a queen from a fairytale, impossible to ignore. Her presence had a hypnotic power, and Mark Antony was not immune to her charm.

When Cleopatra's ship reached the shore, Mark Antony couldn't take his eyes off her. He had called her to discuss political matters, but politics slipped from his mind the moment he saw her. Cleopatra honestly looked like a queen out of a storybook. Her arrival not only surprised everyone but also changed how Antony saw her. In that instant, more than just an alliance was born; a bond stronger than anyone could have imagined tied their fates together forever.

Cleopatra was clever and knew how to use her charm to hold onto her throne. Mark Antony promised to protect her and ensure Egypt's stability. In return, Cleopatra would give him all he needed to achieve his goals in Rome. Together, they formed a pact, helping each other get what they desired. Mark Antony needed Egypt's support to gain more power in Rome, and Cleopatra dreamed of expanding her kingdom beyond the Nile. Their union was not only risky but also the beginning of an adventure that would challenge the mighty power of Rome itself.

As Cleopatra and Mark Antony grew closer and their forces stronger, many in Rome began to worry. To the Romans, Cleopatra wasn't just a foreign queen; she was different—her customs and way of ruling didn't match theirs. Her enemies started spreading rumors, claiming she was a sorceress who had bewitched Antony and pulled him away from his responsibilities. Octavian, Antony's greatest rival, used these stories to make Rome see Cleopatra as a dangerous threat.

But their relationship wasn't just about politics and power. In 40 BC, after Mark Antony returned to Rome, Cleopatra gave birth to twins Alexander Helios and Cleopatra Selene. Their names — Helios and Selene — symbolized the Sun and the Moon, as if fate had destined them to rule a great empire together. Cleopatra dreamed of her children one day inheriting her kingdom and making it even more potent. This dream tied her even closer to Antony; for now, they shared ambitions, a family, and a legacy they were determined to protect.

Despite his duties in Rome, Antony returned to Egypt, drawn more and more into Cleopatra's world. According to some accounts, they married by 37 BC, following Egyptian rituals, and blended their identities and kingdoms. Even though the marriage had no legal value in Rome, it symbolized Antony's devotion to Cleopatra and their shared desire to create a united empire.

Rome Faces Cleopatra and Mark Antony

Cleopatra and Mark Antony became a powerful team, an unstoppable alliance. Together, they ruled their lands with the dream of making them more prominent and more prosperous. But soon, their strength would be put to the test, for many in Rome saw them as a threat. To the Roman leaders, they were not just a man and a woman bound by fate — they were a danger that could challenge the power of mighty Rome.

Octavian, Rome's powerful consul, decided to face Mark Antony and Cleopatra. He wanted to rule without rivals, so he told everyone that Mark Antony was no longer a great general, that he had betrayed Rome and become a weak man seduced by Egypt's luxuries. He also claimed that Cleopatra was not a wise and brave queen but a cunning sorceress who had lured Antony away from his duties. With these lies, Octavian convinced Rome that they must fight against them in a battle that would decide the fate of the ancient world.

Taking advantage of the rumors spreading in Rome, Octavian, Antony's greatest enemy, presented himself as a hero to the people. He convinced the Senate and the Roman soldiers that Mark Antony and Cleopatra were a menace. Meanwhile, things became harder and harder for the queen and the general. Little by little, some of Antony's soldiers began to doubt him and abandoned him, weakening his forces when he needed them most.

THE BATTLE OF ACTIUM

The final battle came in 31 B.C., on the sea of Actium. The sun blazed fiercely over the waves as chaos erupted. Ships crashed with a thunderous noise, oars splashed wildly, and the shouts of soldiers filled the air. In the middle of it all, Cleopatra stood firm, her heart pounding like a war drum. She faced a difficult choice: stay by Mark Antony's side or save the future of Egypt. Before her, the battle raged, reminding her of all that was at stake. Despite the courage of her sailors and soldiers, Cleopatra knew deep down that they would lose.

Cleopatra's mind raced. Her heart begged her to stay and fight alongside Mark Antony, but another voice inside her whispered to think of Egypt — of its people, of the pharaohs who had ruled before her, of the future of her land. If she fell in this battle, what would become of Egypt? Her people would lose their queen and their hope.

It pained her to think of leaving Mark Antony behind, but she knew she had to protect her kingdom. Among the screams of sailors and the clash of battle, she made a hard decision that few would understand. She did not flee out of fear but because it was the only way to save what she loved. With a small gesture to her navigator, she ordered a change of course. Her ships began to pull away, vanishing into the smoke and roar of battle.

The sails of her ships filled with wind, carrying her away from the chaos. Cleopatra, her eyes full of tears, looked back and saw everything burning in unstoppable flames. Her heart ached as the scorching sun and the salty breeze reminded her of the harsh reality. She still trusted in Mark Antony's courage and cleverness. But neither of them had foreseen Octavian's cunning or the unstoppable force of his army. Deep inside, Cleopatra hoped that her departure would make Antony stronger. Without her on the battlefield, he would not have to worry about protecting her and could focus entirely on the fight.

Meanwhile, on his ship, Mark Antony fought with all his strength. He watched the horizon, seeing his fleet struggle to hold back defeat. Suddenly, someone shouted:

"Cleopatra's ships are pulling away!"

Octavian was attacking with all his power. Antony's heart sank. He had counted on the Egyptian fleet's support, but now it was leaving, and everything seemed to fall apart around him.

His mind flooded with doubt. Had Cleopatra betrayed him? Had she abandoned him at the worst possible moment? A sharp pain pierced his chest. Confused, he stood still amid the noise and chaos, watching Cleopatra's ships disappear. He remembered when they dreamed of ruling a great empire together, but now, it all seemed like a fading illusion.

Octavian's troops advanced, crushing everything in their path and breaking through the defenses Antony had tried so hard to hold. The clash of swords and the cries of warriors made the battle seem like the end of the world. When Cleopatra's ship retreated, Antony's army crumbled. His soldiers, terrified and hopeless, scattered like leaves in the wind.

Far from the battle, Cleopatra gazed toward Egypt, imagining it as a safe place, far from the storm. The battle was lost, but the fight for her kingdom's destiny was not over. Though her heart ached for leaving Mark Antony behind, the queen reminded herself of who she was — the daughter of the pharaohs, the leader her people needed. In her mind, the towers of Alexandria rose like a lighthouse, guiding Egypt through the darkness of the Roman shadow.

For Cleopatra, this was not the end but the beginning

of a new challenge. Now, the most important thing was to be ready to face Octavian. One thing was sure: she would not let Egypt fall. As the sea calmed after the storm, she thought about how to protect her people and keep hope alive. She remembered the busy markets of Alexandria, the towering pyramids, and the mighty Nile River. Returning home did not mean giving up — it meant preparing for what was to come.

Meanwhile, on the battlefield, Mark Antony could not bear to see Cleopatra leaving. His love for her was stronger than his duty as a general. So, he abandoned the fight and followed her, leaving his men to their fate. It was a decisive moment: he followed her instead of continuing the battle, even if it meant losing everything.

Cleopatra's Last Challenge

Returning to Egypt was difficult for Cleopatra. She felt sad and worried but knew she had to be strong. The defeat at Actium weighed heavily on her mind. From that moment on, every decision she made could change Egypt's future.

Meanwhile, Mark Antony was in serious trouble. He had made many mistakes, and fleeing with Cleopatra made him look disloyal and weak, causing him to lose power.

In Alexandria, Cleopatra prepared to defend her city.

THE BATTLE OF ACTIUM

People whispered, worried about Antony's defeat and Octavian's drawing near. But Cleopatra refused to give in to fear. Antony reminded her that she had the strength and wisdom to make the right choices. Without wasting time, the queen gathered her most loyal advisors and ordered them to strengthen the palace's defenses.

Workers loaded ships with supplies at the docks, ensuring Egypt was ready for whatever was coming. Cleopatra walked among them, inspecting every detail. Her presence alone gave everyone courage. Around her, her most trusted counselors waited for her commands.

"Egypt will not fall," she said firmly. "Mark Antony's defeat does not decide our fate."

Little by little, plans began to take shape. They spoke of strategies, risks, and hope. They knew danger was near, but the story was not over.

As Octavian's army approached, the great city of Alexandria prepared to face him. Cleopatra gave her people hope. With her bravery, she gave them the strength to keep fighting.

They had already lost the war. Mark Antony, her great ally and love, fell into despair and, believing all was lost, took his own life. With his last breath, he asked to see Cleopatra one final time. In her arms, he told her never to stop fighting for Egypt. Though the Romans were strong, Cleopatra had already carved her story into history. She would carry her spirit forward like a light in the darkness forever.

THE LAST BATTLE
OF CLEOPATRA

Cleopatra watched from afar as the Roman soldiers marched forward without stopping, drawing closer with every step. Their armor gleamed under the sun, and the ground trembled beneath them, determined to conquer her beloved land. But Cleopatra was a brave warrior, not one to give up easily. Though fear stirred within her, a flame of courage and determination burned brightly in her heart — a flame no one could extinguish.

As she saw the enemy soldiers approaching, she knew her duty was to protect her people until the end. With every step the Romans took, her resolve grew more assertive. She had to stand tall for Egypt.

Cleopatra strolled through the palace, feeling the heavy weight of responsibility upon her. She knew she had to appear calm and fearless to inspire her people. She wanted her soldiers to see her as strong and brave, for only then would they find the strength to resist Octavian's mighty army.

Suddenly, a terrible silence fell over Alexandria. It was as if the entire city held its breath, waiting for what would come. Cleopatra felt her heart beat faster, realizing the decisive moment had arrived. From her window, the queen watched as the Roman soldiers entered the city step by step. There was no way she could allow herself to be captured. Stories of Octavian's cruel plan echoed in her mind — to parade her through Rome as a trophy, humiliating her before the entire world. That Cleopatra would never allow.

So, Cleopatra made a problematic but heroic decision. She ordered her servants to fetch a small hidden chest. Inside, there was a venomous serpent — a sacred animal in Egypt, a symbol of eternity and power. Cleopatra knew this would be her final act of bravery. She wanted the world to see that she would rather die free than live as a prisoner of the Romans.

Cleopatra prepared herself and reflected in silence: "Will they remember me only as a defeated queen?" No, she thought. She wanted everyone to know she had been brave until the end. She remembered the stories of the ancient pharaohs — great heroes who never surrendered. That was how she wished to be remembered: with respect and admiration.

Then, Cleopatra approached the small chest, where the serpent waited silently. She gazed at it calmly and knew that soon, everything would be over. Yet, she also learned something even more important: even if her life ended there, her courage would live on forever in the stories the Egyptians would tell, generation after generation.

At that moment, time seemed to stand still. Cleopatra felt the warm desert wind enter through the window, carrying the scents of her beloved land.

With serenity, she allowed the serpent to bite her. In her mind, Cleopatra saw beautiful images of Egypt — the golden sunsets over the Nile, the smiling faces of her people, and the grand pyramids rising toward the sky. She knew this was not the end but the beginning of something eternal.

When Octavian's soldiers entered the palace, it was already too late. Cleopatra had chosen her destiny. Octavian had won the battle, but he could not take Cleopatra's freedom, nor could he erase her from the memory of her people. She would live on forever in the hearts of the Egyptians.

In Alexandria, the news spread quickly. Whispers filled the streets, followed by tears and, finally, a quiet sense of pride. Even though the Romans had conquered them, the Egyptians still held onto something no one could take — the strength and example of their brave queen, who had chosen her fate until the very end.

Egypt eventually fell entirely under Roman rule, but Cleopatra became a legend. People remembered her for generations, admiring the story of the queen who stood against Rome until her final breath.

Though Cleopatra was gone, her people never let her memory fade. She lived on in stories, songs sung around the fire, and tales passed down from parents to children. In this way, Cleopatra achieved the impossible—she triumphed even in defeat.

Years passed, and the marks of Rome grew all over Egypt. Yet something remained untouched: the story of Cleopatra, the warrior queen and brave defender of Egypt. Her life became a shining flame in the darkness, a light that inspired young hearts to believe in courage, strength, and dignity.

Even today, when the stars sparkle over Alexandria and the desert wind softly stirs the sands, some say you can hear her voice whispering in the Nile. Cleopatra became an eternal symbol — a queen who never surrendered and who still lives on in the hearts of all who dare to be brave and fight for what they love.

Her story teaches us that courage is not about never falling but rising and moving forward, even when all seems lost. Cleopatra left the world this everlasting lesson, written in the golden sands of Egypt — a story that will never fade, for great heroes never die completely; they live on forever in the hearts of those who remember them.

EPILOGUE
A LEGACY NEVER FORGOTTEN

The old storyteller still sat beneath the shade of Alexandria's ancient columns, surrounded by the children who had come to hear his tale at dawn. Now, the sun was sinking behind the horizon, painting the sky in shades of gold and crimson. The breeze carried the salty scent of the Mediterranean and the sweet aroma of spices from the marketplace. The sun was setting, but the storyteller still had a few final words.

The children gazed at the old man, their eyes wide with wonder, still thrilled by the story they had just heard. Through his words, they had traveled across time. They had seen mighty armies march, felt the clash of battles, and witnessed the fall of a queen who never gave up.

The old storyteller remained silent momentarily, letting the children absorb the tale. Then, with a steady and solemn voice, he asked his final question:

"Tell me, little ones... Was Cleopatra just a queen? Or was she the last great Pharaoh of Egypt?"

The children looked at one another. Cleopatra had been many things: a ruler, a strategist, a brave warrior. She had stood against Rome until the very end, refusing to surrender. And though she had lost her kingdom and her life, her story remained alive.

At last, a girl with dark curls and a fierce gaze dared to answer:

"She was more than a queen," she said softly. "She never gave up. Even though Rome defeated her, she was still a winner."

The old man nodded slowly, a proud smile lighting up his face.

"Yes," he said. "Though Rome won the battle, the legend of Cleopatra will live forever."

The children sat in thoughtful silence for a moment longer. Then, one by one, they began to rise. Their minds were filled with images of golden palaces, burning ships, and a queen who, with her head held high, had defied an empire. The story had ended, but something within them had changed.

The old storyteller watched them leave as the

EPILOGUE: A LEGACY NEVER FORGOTTEN

sun disappeared beyond the horizon. Night gently embraced Alexandria, and the sky turned deep blue and violet. One by one, the stars appeared, twinkling just as they had centuries ago over Cleopatra's Egypt.

And then, in the hush of the night breeze, a distant whisper echoed — a sound that even time itself could not silence:

"I am still the Pharaoh."

DID YOU ENJOY THIS STORY?

In the next pages, you'll find extra content and valuable information. But first…

If you found this book interesting or inspiring, please consider leaving a review. It's quick and easy!

It only takes a minute, but it means the world to us — it helps more children and families discover this story and allows us to keep creating books like this one.

Your opinion is worth gold.
Thank you so much for your support!

FUN FACTS ABOUT CLEOPATRA

Things you probably didn't know about the last great queen of Egypt

1. **She wasn't Egyptian by origin**
   Cleopatra was born in Alexandria, Egypt, but her family, the Ptolemies, were actually Greek. They came to Egypt after Alexander the Great's conquest and ruled the country for many years.
2. **She spoke many languages**
   It is said that Cleopatra spoke more than seven languages, including Greek, Egyptian, Hebrew, and Aramaic. She was a real polyglot!
3. **She was the first of her family to speak Egyptian**
   No Ptolemaic king before her had ever learned the Egyptian language. Cleopatra was the first to speak directly to her people.
4. **She was brilliant**
   Cleopatra had an excellent education. She studied mathematics, astronomy, philosophy, politics, and literature. People admired her more for her intelligence and charisma than for her beauty.

5. **She ruled with her brothers**
   Egyptian law at the time forced Cleopatra to share the throne with her brothers, but she made most of the important decisions.
6. **She surprised Julius Caesar**
   According to legend, Cleopatra secretly met Julius Caesar by being rolled up inside a carpet. The servants unrolled the rug, and there she was — ready to make an alliance!
7. **She had children with two famous Romans**
   Cleopatra had a son with Julius Caesar, named Caesarion. Later, she had three children with Mark Antony: Alexander Helios, Cleopatra Selene, and Ptolemy Philadelphus.
8. **She was a great leader in difficult times**
   Cleopatra ruled Egypt during one of its most challenging periods, which was filled with wars and betrayals. Yet, she always defended her country with intelligence and courage.
9. **Her death is still a mystery**
   Some say Cleopatra allowed a poisonous snake to bite her, while others believe someone secretly poisoned her. No one knows for sure.
10. **She is one of the most famous women in history**
    More than 2,000 years after her death, people still remember Cleopatra in books, movies, songs, and plays. She remains a true eternal legend!

CLEOPATRA'S TIMELINE

The most critical moments of her life

69 BC (0 years old)
Cleopatra is born in Alexandria, Egypt, as part of the Ptolemaic dynasty.

51 BC (18 years old)
She becomes queen alongside her younger brother, Ptolemy XIII.

48 BC (21 years old)
Cleopatra meets Julius Caesar and allies to reclaim her throne.

47 BC (22 years old)
Her son Caesarion is born, son of Cleopatra and Julius Caesar.

44 BC (25 years old)
Julius Caesar is assassinated. Cleopatra returns to Egypt with Caesarion.

41 BC (28 years old)
She meets Mark Antony, one of the most potent Roman generals, and they ally.

40 BC (29 years old)
Cleopatra and Mark Antony have twins: Alexander Helios and Cleopatra Selene.

31 BC (38 years old)
Cleopatra and Mark Antony lose the famous naval Battle of Actium against Octavian.

30 BC (39 years old)
Cleopatra dies in Alexandria. Egypt becomes part of the Roman Empire.

QUESTIONS TO REFLECT AND DISCUSS

After reading Cleopatra's story, take a moment to think about these questions. There are no right or wrong answers — the most important thing is to reflect.

1. What qualities made Cleopatra a good leader?
2. Do you think she was brave when facing Rome? Why?
3. Would you have made the same decisions if you were in her place?
4. What do you think was the most challenging moment in her life?
5. What did you learn about power, strategy, and intelligence by reading her story?
6. Why do you think people still remember Cleopatra after so many centuries?
7. Would you like to be a leader someday? What kind of leader would you be?
8. What does "writing your destiny" mean to you, as Cleopatra did?

CLEOPATRA'S MINI GLOSSARY

Learn the key words from the story

Alliance
A strong agreement between two people, groups, or countries to help each other.
Example: Cleopatra made an alliance with Julius Caesar.

Battle
A big fight between two armies.
Example: The Battle of Actium was Cleopatra's last great fight.

Betrayal
When someone you trust goes against you or deceives you.
Example: Cleopatra often faced betrayal from people close to her.

Conquer
To take control of a place or people, often by force.
Example: Rome tried to conquer Egypt.

Dynasty
A family that rules a country for many generations.
Example: Cleopatra belonged to the Ptolemaic dynasty.

Exile
When someone is forced to leave their country and live far away.
Example: Cleopatra and her sister escaped into exile.

Legacy
Something important a person leaves behind to be remembered by future generations.
Example: Cleopatra's legacy lasted for more than 2,000 years.

Nomads
People who travel from place to place without a permanent home.
Example: Cleopatra learned from the Bedouin nomads in the desert.

Pharaoh
The king or queen of ancient Egypt, believed to be both a ruler and a god.

CLEOPATRA'S MINI GLOSSARY

Strategy
A smart plan to achieve a goal or win a battle.
Example: Cleopatra always used strategy to face her enemies.

Throne
The royal seat of a king or queen. It also means the right or power to rule.
Example: Cleopatra fought to recover her throne.

REFERENCES

Bianchi, B. (2023). *Cleopatra the Great: Last Power of the Ptolemaic Dynasty*. ARCE; American Research Center in Egypt. https://arce.org/resource/cleopatra-great-last-power-ptolemaic-dynasty/

Devereaux, B. (2023, May 26). *Collections: On the Reign of Cleopatra*. A Collection of Unmitigated Pedantry. https://acoup.blog/2023/05/26/collections-on-the-reign-of-cleopatra/comment-page-1/

The Project Gutenberg eBook of History of Cleopatra, Queen of Egypt, by Jacob Abbott. (2025). Gutenberg.org. https://www.gutenberg.org/files/40205/40205-h/40205-h.htm

Watkins, T. (2020). *The Timeline of the Life of Cleopatra*. Sjsu.edu. https://www.sjsu.edu/faculty/watkins/cleopatra.htm

Books at On Military Matters. (2025). Onmilitarymatters.com. https://www.onmilitarymatters.com/dfcatalog.php?period=1200

Edward, G. (2023). *North Africa and the desert*. Gutenberg.org. https://www.gutenberg.org/ebooks/70171.html.images

History.com Editors. (2009, November 9). *Cleopatra*. HISTORY; A&E Television Networks.

https://www.history.com/topics/ancient-egypt/cleopatra

The Ptolemies of Egypt. (n.d.). Nabataea.net. https://nabataea.net/explore/history/ptolomy/

Bianchi, B. (2023). *Cleopatra the Great: Last Power of the Ptolemaic Dynasty.* ARCE; American Research Center in Egypt. https://arce.org/resource/cleopatra-great-last-power-ptolemaic-dynasty/

Cushion, H. (2024, August 8). *The Relationship Between Julius Caesar and Cleopatra: A Historical Overview.* Joditaylorbooks.com; Jodi Taylor Books. https://www.joditaylorbooks.com/p/the-relationship-between-julius-caesar

History of Cleopatra, queen of Egypt. (2025). Ufl.edu. https://original-ufdc.uflib.ufl.edu/UF00001908/00001

The Project Gutenberg eBook of The Life and Times of Cleopatra, Queen of Egypt, by Arthur E. P. Brome Weigall. (2025). Gutenberg.org. https://www.gutenberg.org/files/54038/54038-h/54038-h.htm

Cleopatra | Book Summary. (2024). Swiftread.com. https://swiftread.com/books/cleopatra

History.com Editors. (2009, November 9). *Cleopatra.* HISTORY; A&E Television Networks. https://www.history.com/topics/ancient-egypt/cleopatra

Tyldesley, J. (2019). *Cleopatra.* Encyclopædia Britannica. https://www.britannica.com/biography/Cleopatra-queen-of-Egypt

REFERENCES

Ferguson, R. J. (2024). *Octavian, Antony and Cleopatra: Propaganda and war*. ResearchGate. Retrieved from https://www.researchgate.net/publication/383565605_Octavian_Antony_and_Cleopatra_Propaganda_and_War

History.com Editors. (2009, November 9). *Cleopatra*. HISTORY; A&E Television Networks. https://www.history.com/topics/ancient-egypt/cleopatra

The Editors of Encyclopedia Britannica. (2018, April 2). *Battle of Actium | ancient Roman history*. Encyclopædia Britannica. https://www.britannica.com/event/Battle-of-Actium-ancient-Roman-history

Visiting Contributor. (2021, December 20). *The Alliance between Marcus Antoninus and Cleopatra VII*. The Roman Empire. https://roman-empire.net/republic/mark-antony-and-cleopatra-alliance

History.com Editors. (2018, August 21). *The Battle of Actium*. HISTORY; A&E Television Networks. https://www.history.com/this-day-in-history/the-battle-of-actium

Nutt, D. (2022, March 15). *Historian delves into the battle that shaped the Roman Empire*. Cornell Chronicle. https://news.cornell.edu/stories/2022/03/historian-delves-battle-shaped-roman-empire

The Editors of Encyclopedia Britannica. (2018, April 2). *Battle of Actium | ancient Roman history*. Encyclopædia Britannica. https://www.britannica.com/event/Battle-of-Actium-ancient-Roman-history

Fischer-Bovet, C. (2015). *Cleopatra VII, 69–30 BCE. Oxford Classical Dictionary.* https://doi.org/10.1093/acrefore/9780199381135.013.1672

Herdman, J. (2021, May 6). *Questions in Egyptology 9: The Death of Cleopatra - Julia Herdman Books.* Julia Herdman Books. https://juliaherdman.com/2021/05/06/the-death-of-cleopatra/

Kleiner, D. E. E. (2005). *Cleopatra and Rome.* JSTOR; Harvard University Press. https://www.jstor.org/stable/j.ctv1q3z29z

The Death of Cleopatra. (n.d.). Smithsonian Institution. https://www.si.edu/object/death-cleopatra%3Asaam_1994.17

www.ingramcontent.com/pod-product-compliance
Lightning Source LLC
LaVergne TN
LVHW012047070526
838201LV00082B/3796